A Robbie Reader

Philo Farnsworth

INVENTS TV

by
Russell Roberts

Mitchell Lane
PUBLISHERS

P.O. Box 196
Hockessin, Delaware 19707
Visit us on the web: www.mitchelllane.com
Comments? email us: mitchelllane@mitchelllane.com

Printing   1   2   3   4   5   6   7   8   9

A Robbie Reader

Hillary Duff	Thomas Edison	Albert Einstein
Philo Farnsworth	Henry Ford	Robert Goddard
Mia Hamm	Tony Hawk	LeBron James
Donovan McNabb	Dr. Seuss	Charles Schulz

Library of Congress Cataloging-in-Publication Data
Roberts, Russell, 1953-
    Philo Farnsworth Invents TV / by Russell Roberts.
        p. cm. — (A Robbie reader)
    Includes bibliographical references and index.
    ISBN 1-58415-303-2 (library bound)
    1. Farnsworth, Philo Taylor, 1906-1971—Juvenile literature. 2. Electric engineers—United States—Biography—Juvenile literature. 3. Inventors—Unites States—Biography—Juvenile literature. 4. Television—History—Juvenile literature. I. Title. II. Series.
    TK6635.F3R63 2004b
    621.388'092--dc22
                                                                                                2004009302

ABOUT THE AUTHOR: Russell Roberts has written and published books on a variety of subjects, including *Ten Days to a Sharper Memory, Discover the Hidden New Jersey,* and *Stolen! A History of Base Stealing.* He also wrote *Pedro Menendez de Aviles* and *Philo T. Farnsworth: The Life of Television's Forgotten Inventor* for Mitchell Lane. He lives in Bordentown, New Jersey with his family and a remarkably lazy, yet fiesty calico cat named Rusti.

PHOTO CREDITS: Cover, p. 4, 6, 8 (top), 8 (bottom), 10, 12, 20, 22, 26, 28 University of Utah; p. 14 philotfarnsworth.com; p. 16 Corbis; p. 18 Hulton/Archive

ACKNOWLEDGMENTS: The following story has been thoroughly researched, and to the best of our knowledge, represents a true story. While every possible effort has been made to ensure accuracy, the publisher will not assume liability for damages caused by inaccuracies in the data, and makes no warranty on the accuracy of the information contained herein. This story has not been authorized nor endorsed by anyone associated with Philo Farnsworth's estate.

TABLE OF CONTENTS

At age 13, Philo had already won a prize for one of his inventions.

ROWS OF HAY

One day in 1921, Philo (FY-low) Taylor Farnsworth was cutting hay on a farm. But his mind was not on his work. Instead he was thinking about an **invention**.

Philo often thought about inventions while doing farm chores. He had already invented a few things. One was a way to use magnets to stop thieves from stealing cars. He won a prize for this invention.

He looked at the hay he had just cut. It had fallen to the ground in neat rows. Each row lay on top of another.

The rows gave him an idea for two inventions. They would work like your eye and

Philo, at age 17, had solved a problem that many others could not–how to send sounds and pictures through the air by electricity.

brain. One would look at things like an eye. The other would **decode** those things like a brain. They would both work in rows, like the rows of cut hay. The eye part would scan an image in rows, from top to bottom, top to bottom. It would change what it saw into electrical signals. The brain part would change those signals back into rows, which would form a picture.

Philo had just figured out how a television would work and he was only 15 years old.

Sometimes Lewis Farnsworth, Philo's father, shown here, helped him with his science experiments.

This was Philo's hometown in Utah.

A SMART BOY

Philo was born on August 19, 1906, on a farm in Utah. His parents were Lewis and Serena Farnsworth. Lewis always wanted to find better work or a bigger farm, so the family moved many times.

Philo loved animals. On one farm he had a pony. On another farm he had a flock of lambs. He also liked music and he played the violin in a dance band.

But science was his first love. He liked to know how things worked. Philo took apart anything he could find, such as **generators** and alarm clocks. Once he found an old electric motor. He hated to wash clothes in his mother's

Even as a young man, Philo's dreams always included television.

hand-operated machine. He hooked up the motor to the washing machine and no longer had to turn the crank by hand.

In high school Philo met a science teacher named Justin Tolman. He and Tolman would stay after school working on science problems. Sometimes they stayed so late the janitor got mad!

Philo wanted to invent television. This idea was not new. Other people had tried to invent TV, but their pictures were always blurry.

The first TVs used moving parts. Philo wanted to use electricity to make TV work. He thought it would be the best way to send pictures and sound through the air.

One day, Tolman saw that Philo had covered the blackboard with drawings and math problems. Tolman asked Philo what everything meant. Philo said that it was his ideas on how to invent television. He showed Tolman his ideas and Tolman thought they were good.

Philo, working on a television-related problem in the 1930s.

Philo kept studying and thinking about TV. He got a job and started dating a girl named Elma. Her nickname was Pem.

When Philo's father died on January 28, 1924, Philo had to support his family. He did not have any more time to study or work on inventing TV. This upset him. He knew others were also trying to invent TV and he worried they would do it first.

What could he do?

This photo of Elma "Pem" Gardner, Philo's wife, was taken in 1936.

A BIG BREAK

In the spring of 1926, Philo was living in Salt Lake City, Utah. He now called himself Phil. He was still trying to invent TV, but he was getting nowhere.

About this time, he met a man named George Everson. When Phil was able to fix a tricky problem in Everson's car, Everson realized that Phil was very smart. This was Phil's big break. Everson gave him $6,000 to build a TV.

This was a great time in Phil's life. He married Pem, and they moved to California. Phil made a TV lab in his home. His neighbors did not know what he was doing. They thought he might be breaking the law. They even called the police!

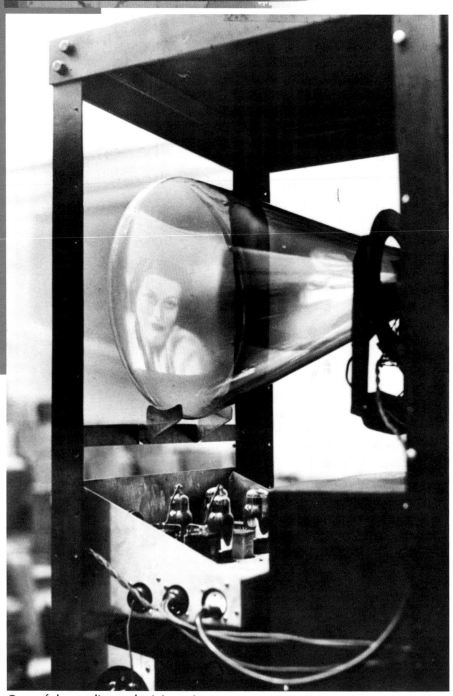

One of the earliest television pictures.

Phil tried many experiments (ek-SPEER-uh-ments). One time, he thought he had everything just right. He plugged in his machine—and it blew up!

But he kept trying. Finally he sent a picture from one room to another using electricity. The date was September 7, 1927. "That's it, folks," he said. "We've done it."

Phil and his friends were happy that they had gotten this far. But the picture was very small. Phil knew that he still had a lot of work to do.

In 1929, Phil's first child, Philo Jr., was born. Eventually he and Pem had four children: Philo Jr., Kenneth, born in 1931, Russell, born in 1935, and Kent, born in 1948.

Others were also working on TV. One was Vladimir Zworykin (VLAD-ih-meer ZVOR-ih-ken), a scientist who worked for a big company called the Radio Corporation of America (RCA). The company had lots of money.

Pem helped Phil whenever she could.

Phil did not have lots of money. It was expensive to do all those experiments. Phil worried that RCA would invent a working TV first. Both Phil and RCA knew that people would like TV, and that TV would make a lot of money.

Phil tried to find more money for his work. But it was hard. He and Pem moved to Philadelphia. There Phil worked for a company called Philco. Together they made TV shows. They were not like anything on TV today. The shows were black-and-white cartoons.

But other companies were also making TV shows.

Math is very important for scientists and inventors. Here Phil uses his math skills to solve a problem.

TROUBLES

In 1932, Phil and Pem's second son Kenny died. He was just one year old. Phil and Pem wanted to take him back to Utah to bury him, but Philco would not let Phil take time off to go. They said he had to stay and work. Phil was angry. In 1933 he left Philco and started his own company.

Now Phil had to face RCA by himself. He tried making his own TV shows. But RCA did the same thing. Phil also had legal problems with RCA. Phil had patents (PAT-ents) on his inventions. Patents protect an inventor by making it illegal for anyone to copy an invention without permission. But they only last for a few years. If RCA could delay paying Phil

Phil improving the picture on one of his early televisions.

for the ideas in his patents, then Phil would never be paid for all his hard work.

Phil was tired and worn down from worrying. He lost weight. He drank too much alcohol. He was nervous and upset much of the time.

In December 1941, the United States entered World War II. All work on TV stopped. It was more important to win the war than to continue with inventions for the home.

Phil had many health problems and was not well. Time was running out on his patents. He took up smoking. He finally went to the hospital and slowly got better. But he still had troubles in his life. His brother died in a plane crash. A fire burned his house down.

When the war ended, RCA started working on TV again. They built TV sets that could fit in people's living rooms. People did like TV. They liked watching TV shows in their homes. Soon many people had RCA TV sets.

Finally Phil sold his company. RCA had won the TV battle.

Trying to invent television kept Phil constantly busy.

LAST YEARS

After Phil sold his company, whenever he thought about television, he got angry and sad. He blamed television for his troubles. He did not even want to hear the word "television." But sometimes he did watch television. One of these times was when he watched as Neil Armstrong became the first person to walk on the moon on July 20, 1969.

Phil worked on other inventions for the rest of his life. He died of **pneumonia** (nuh-MOW-nya) on March 11, 1974. Would anyone remember his work on TV?

People did remember. The U.S. Postal Service put his picture on a stamp. He was recognized as an important inventor by *Time*

This statue of Phil as a young boy, dreaming about television, is located in Washington, D.C.

magazine. A mountain in Utah was named after him, and a large television **antenna** was put on top of it.

Today there is a statue of Phil in Washington, D.C. It shows him holding one of his inventions and calls him the Father of Television. The people who see the statue know he was a great inventor.

Phil would be happy.

This early Farnsworth television is much different from the televisions of today.

1906 Born on August 19 in Beaver City, Utah
1921 While cutting hay, figures out how television could work
1922 Explains about television to science teacher Justin Tolman
1924 Father dies on January 28
1926 Meets George Everson, who gives him money to build first television
1926 Marries Elma "Pem" Gardner on May 27
1927 Sends first television picture using electricity on September 7
1929 Son Philo, Jr. born September 23
1931 Son Kenneth born January 15
1932 Young son Kenny dies on March 7
1935 Son Russell born on October 9
1948 Son Kent born on September 4
1949 Sells his company
1971 Dies on March 11

FIND OUT MORE

Books

Kent, Zachary. *The Story of Television.* Chicago: Children's Press, Inc., 1990.

McPherson, Stephanie Sammartino. *TV's Forgotten Hero: The Story of Philo Farnsworth.* Minneapolis: Carolrhoda Books, Inc., 1996.

Roberts, Russell. *Philo T. Farnsworth: The Life of Television's Forgotten Inventor.* Hockessin, Del.: Mitchell Lane Publishers, Inc., 2004.

Web Addresses

Philo T. Farnsworth Archives, Official Site
http://philotfarnsworth.com

Philo T. Farnsworth Collection, J. Willard Marriott Library, University of Utah
www.lib.utah.edu/spc/photo/p437/p437.html

Television History–The First 75 Years "Early Television Experiments–Philo T. Farnsworth"
www.tvhistory.tv/Philo.htm

The Farnovision
www.farnovision.com

Antenna (an-TEN-uh)—Something that receives signals.

Decode (dee-KODE)—Turning something back into its
original form.

Generator (JEN-er-AY-tor)—A machine that takes one form of
energy and turns it into another.

Invention (in-VEN-shun)—Making something that did not
previously exist.

Pneumonia (nuh-MOW-nya)—a disease of the lungs.